Into the Stillness

Poems by Jackie Magnuson Ash

Kansas City Spartan Press Missouri

Spartan Press
Kansas City, Missouri
spartanpresskc.com

Copyright (c) Jackie Magnuson Ash, 2018
First Edition 1 3 5 7 9 10 8 6 4 2
ISBN: 978-1-946642-79-0
LCCN: 2018961885

Design, edits and layout: Jason Ryberg
Cover and title page image: Jon Lee Grafton
Author photo: Bob Ash
All rights reserved. No part of this publication may be reproduced or transmitted in any form or by any means, electronic or mechanical, including photocopying, recording or by info retrieval system, without prior written permission from the author.

Spartan Press would like to thank Prospero's Books, The Fellowship of N-finite Jest, The Prospero Institute of Disquieted P/o/e/t/i/c/s, Will Leathem, Tom Wayne, Jeanette Powers, j. d. tulloch, Jon Bidwell, Jason Preu, Mark McClane, Tony Hayden and the whole Osage Arts Community.

The author extends her thanks to Patricia and the original members of Prairie Poets and Writers; to Bev, Margaret, Judy, Chris, Garry, Ann, Mary; to Lori, who goes above and beyond, and to Jason. Heartfelt thanks to my husband Bob, daughter Stacy, son Tyler (and Sarah and the girls), and to my sisters Judy, Jill, Janelle.

Notes:

The man in "Who Will Listen?" is based on Wes Jackson of The Land Institute, Salina, Kansas, and the author's memory of one of his lectures. Any errors in content are the author's.

The Louise Erdrich quote in "New Year's Day Hike at Kanopolis Reservoir" comes from her novel *The Plague of Doves*.

CONTENTS

Cause and Effect / 1

Coming Home 1968 / 2

Honeymoon Hike / 3

Graduation / 4

First Child / 5

April Fools / 6

A Prairie Summer / 7

Season's End / 8

Unwanted Gifts / 9

Machine Shop / 10

Makeshift / 11

First Fall / 12

When June Comes Round / 13

At the Core of the Universe / 14

A Road Between / 15

Doorway / 17

There Comes a Time / 19

Grief's Edge / 20

Sunday Chores / 21

The Land / 23

The A-C 190XT / 24

How It Is Right Now / 25

Apart from Everything Else: Migraine / 27

Her husband asks / 28

Amid Blessings / 29

Who Will Listen? / 30

Prairie Eventide / 32

Weed Trouble / 33

Balancing the Ledger / 34

Of an Autumn Afternoon / 35

Sometimes Truth / 36

The Supplanter / 37

Where a Familiar Ache Rides / 38

Half Bitter, Half Sweet / 39

Taking Note / 40

Something More / 41

A Certain Solace / 42

To Have and to Hold / 44

Deep in the Afternoon / 45

Place and People / 46

December's End / 48

Ice Storm / 49

When Stars Are More than Stars / 50

New Year's Day Hike at Kanopolis / 51

Homebound / 53

Precious with History / 55

Rotating Fields / 56

Morning Coffee / 58

Epilogue: Cottonwood 2018 / 60

In memory of my parents
Charles and Maxine (Clark) Magnuson

Cause and Effect

. . . by looking narrowly, you shall see there was no luck in the matter,
but it was all a problem in arithmetic, or an experiment in chemistry.
– Emerson

It wasn't luck she once had a crush on him,
he once lusted after her, or so he said,
later, when he knew her better. He
made her laugh. She made him dinner.

And then there came an ordinary Sunday:
he lay stretched on her brocade couch,
lost to *60 Minutes,* maybe, or a ballgame;
she sat lotus-style in the armchair,
awake to their emerging certainty.

The proof of them remains, even when
one of them sulks, the other accuses.
Love gathers in children, shared
days and nights, aging minds.

She makes him laugh. He makes her dinner.
They give each other wine and flowers
and say it wasn't luck that brought them here.

Coming Home 1968

That first semester he sometimes brings her home.
Her folks are on the way to his folks, if he drives
a certain route. Tonight, he switches off his red Chevy
in front of her house. Snow glistens, stars glitter.

She steps from the car, catches a whiff of silage, and a
late September day stirs inside her, when she roamed
off campus, homesick for deer paths and goldenrod.
Smack! A snowball collides with her head. Before
he can throw another, she scrambles up the walk to
scoop and mold her own. By the time they reach the
front door, their laughter rings in the stillness. She
tumbles into the house. Her mother grips a dishtowel,
stares at her from the dining room. Her dad leans forward
in his chair. *It's just me,* she says and steps into
the dark again.

At the car, he fills her arms with her things. *If you're
lucky, you'll see me again,* he says, brushing her shoulder,
her hair, as if he saw snow there. After his car lights
disappear over the county bridge, she lingers in
the night's glimmer, suitcase at her feet. The crown of
the farm's old cottonwood rises above the other creek
trees, its black against a snow globe of stars. The tree speaks
to her of roots; the stars, of journeys.

Honeymoon Hike

The newlyweds perch on a boulder,
catching their breath, scanning
the Guadalupe Mountains—
bone white, bleached green—
rimming the desert below. They joke
about the trailhead sign. One Mile,
it said. *One mile straight up,* they say.

The naked trail tilts and twists,
as the young couple trudges on.
Sun scorches the air, vistas widen—
switch—back—switch—back.
If only she'd complain. She doesn't.
He minds his feet sheathed in
flimsy canvas—step up, up again.

The mountain crest nears. They
glimpse a pine, then another.
The path flattens, and silver trunks
crowd round and dwarf them.
She sinks to a slab of stone,
a spent pilgrim, silenced
by a whispery holy place.

Neither wants to face the slide
back down this unexpected mountain.
They lunch on apples, sweet pudding.
He dreams of sleeping under the stars.

Graduation

A robin lands in the yard, then another, and another,
late sunshine lighting up bugs and seeds in the grass. One
plucks a clump of dead clippings and flies up to her nest.
He watches from the porch, an after-work beer in his hand.

He didn't expect his first job after graduation to bring
him home again. The reason it did: his father-in-law
had open-heart surgery and needed someone to farm
for a season. Being the only son-in-law who wasn't
already working, the family asked him to do it. When he
agreed, he was in the final whirl of papers, tests, projects.
While his father-in-law healed, he worked the fields and
mailed out resumes. The result was only one offer, not in
Colorado or Missouri or New Mexico but right here in
the middle of Kansas; not the professional position he
anticipated but a foot-in-the-door job. After fall harvest,
he and his wife moved to town, into a house his parents
own, the one attached to the porch he's sitting on.
A wistfulness slides down his throat with the beer. It's been
a year since his last stroll across the university quad.

Birds flap and flutter as his wife, home from the doctor,
turns the car into the drive. He waves. It occurs to him it
never again will be just the two of them.

First Child

Life gathers inside her
swells her breasts and belly
in gentle measure.

While weeding the garden
or hanging curtains,
she senses the wisdom
her body holds but keeps
secret, like Earth Herself
guarding sacred mystery.

She often bows her head
in the hush of a sultry afternoon
and places her palm against
the tremor that is her baby.

April Fools

Down the backyard a ways green clumps of slender leaves catch her eye. This year, she knows what they are. Last year they wilted and vanished by June, and she forgot about them, busy with a small son and a new home. Weeks later on a quiet July morning, delicate bouquets of pink lilies, tall, stalk-naked, stood where bare ground had been. How odd they were, how sneaky.

Around the time those clumps faded, she began to blossom, pregnant again, just weeks after her husband had started a better job and they'd bought a two-bedroom bungalow. Though they were planning on a second child, they weren't expecting it so soon. Mother Nature decided otherwise. The joy of having a girl, a baby sister for their little boy, washes through her. No more surprises. They're complete, they've rooted.

The children nap inside the house. She sits on the porch steps, keeping an ear tuned toward any stirrings. The back door stands open, and all the windows. Smells rise in the sun-drenched air—warmed brick and soil, her sweaty skin. It's too hot for April. The yard's big elm arches its branches over the patio. With only a hint of leaves, the tree isn't ready to shade her. Mother Nature plays yet another joke. A bumble bee drones by.

A Prairie Summer

Skin and soil parch, plaster
breaks from its lath, sky
bears down like hot iron,
and at night darkness
gathers too close. Everyone
dreams of mountaintops,
tier upon tier, envisions
anywhere but here—this
grassland excessiveness,
where bluster and sun
grind labor into dust.

Season's End

What happened was this: After her dad finished
unloading the final load of milo, he shut off the
combine's engine, climbed out to sit on its metal
landing, closed his eyes, and there they waited for
him—sister, dad, Uncle Louie, floating against
darkness, standing in the order of their deaths.
His booted feet rested on a ladder rung, hands
going slack in his lap, head leaning against the
railing, his soiled felt hat tipped off center. From
the foot of the ladder, her mom called his name.
An October breeze lifted fodder into the air.
She called again. After a third time—it was more of a
shout—he awoke. Climbing down the ladder, he said
nothing of the vision, not then. For the next week he
went on with end-of-season chores. Just after sunup
one morning, he couldn't get out of bed, couldn't
move at all. An ambulance sirened him into town.

He's frail now, an old man at 63.

Unwanted Gifts

I don't think you'll be happy as a farmwife.

Her mother says this as they stand together in the farm house kitchen. The kids snack at the old Formica table, warm Pop Tarts sweetening the air.

That her mother speaks from experience is understood. A question circles at the back of her mind: *Mother wasn't happy all those years?* All she can think to say in return is, *I can't tell him not to farm.*

Her husband is about to quit his job and a boss he doesn't like so he can take over the family business. She feels no resistance to this, even though she never considered farming before the stroke felled her father. In fact, she feels a sense of doing something noble, of stepping up to save the family place. Her mother's doubts annoy her.

After brushing crumbs from the counter and hushing her kids, she sees how worn out her mother is. That's where these words spring from: weariness. She decides to tuck them away, like small unwanted gifts.

Machine Shop

It was built by his father-in-law
after the war from bits and pieces
of Camp Phillips—salvaged windows
and beams, penny-a-piece cinder blocks.
He loves the smell: grease smeared
many times over on axles and gears,
translucent oil poured into countless
engines. He runs his hands across
blackened branding irons, brittle
saddles, a worn wooden chest.
Ah, and here are the pieces
of the make-and-break engine,
the one his father-in-law as a boy
listened for at night, at his window.
It chugged at the well with just
enough gas to pump just
enough water to fill to the rim
the old wooden horse tank.
Ch-ch-ch-ch-pop—He sees
the boy in bed, eyes heavy,
wanting to stay awake until
the engine sputters and stops.

This story was slipped in amid
farm talk—other stories too,
poured like oil, rich and seasoned.

Makeshift

The tin-skirted house, doublewide,
well-used, glinty in the sun, now sits
in a brome field across the creek.
On this clean-skied day she kneels
at the edge of plowed ground to take
a picture, not of the makeshift house
but of the landscape. Her boy darts
into the field, onto turned earth
and faces the camera square,
hair the color of sunshine. Her girl,
toddler plump, halts on uneven clods,
frowns, wants to be where her brother is.

The co-op elevator pins the distance.
It's the only village stake. The tiny church
burned years ago. Nellie's store has closed.

Nellie said to her mother yesterday,
I see your daughter hung her curtains.
The trailer is now officially a home.

In the field her children wait, obedient,
watch her snap the shutter, draw them in.

First Fall

The smell of fuel and oil permeates the air. Just beneath it, a hint of fresh earth. From the open-air seat of the idling tractor, he gazes at the field, the last one planted. He drilled the wheat as straight as he could, taking care to keep sight of his mark at the end of the first pass, just as his father-in-law taught him.

He reaches for the gearshift, foot pressing down on the clutch, but stops mid motion. A fox has darted out from trees along the road. It angles across the field toward the river. As it gets closer, he sees a tinge of red on its gray fur, sees also a neon green tennis ball in its mouth. What dog did it steal that from? Don't the Plains Indians call the fox the Trickster, or is that just the coyote? Is this an omen? He laughs at himself. The fox runs on past, ignoring the tractor, and disappears over a rise in the ground.

In the direction of home, sky above yellowing cottonwoods has deepened into a blue-violet promise of rain. Seed is in the ground, and next June will bring his harvest.

When June Comes Round

Hailstones bounce and ping, gather like snow
in the yard and beyond it, in the pale, ripe field.
Husband and wife stand at the picture window
of the trailer-house, dazed by the hammering riot.

On it goes. Brittle stems break, grain shatters.
Need stings the backs of their necks: a trip to
the dentist, new clothes for the kids. Debt
strikes over and over: co-op, machinery, bank.

Our first wheat crop, she says, *like Dad's
first bull. Remember he told us lightning
killed it, in the pasture?* Her husband nods.

They can only think the Universe,
when it detects new order, tests the nerves
of rookies. The din of the storm, the
unforgiving bombardment, does just that.

At the Core of the Universe

There is randomness among the atoms

Her kids circle the yard, chasing
lightening bugs. She sits at
their center with a jar, its lid
hole-punched. Bullfrogs croon
at the pond; on a breeze,
a hint of ripe alfalfa.

Life follows a certain arc—
children, ponds, alfalfa—
yet isn't as she expected.
Measured routine gets
interrupted, plans disrupted,
and at times the unforeseen
brings a startling harshness
to her voice.

Out of the dark,
kids rush up, smelling of
musky sweat. They uncup
elfin hands, spilling glimmers
into the jar on off on off—
Two fireflies blink like electrons
around their nucleus here there—

She praises her little ones
for being gentle with something
so fragile. They dash away,
begin to circle again.

A Road Between

Out of the blue Mrs. Frost calls. The Frost house and
pasture are for sale. Are she and her husband interested?

The Frost farm is adjacent to their farm and once belonged
to her great grandparents, then her great uncle Eric.
Her dad grew up thinking he would own both farms
someday. Back then, a field road lay between the two
properties, an artery connecting her grandmother to two
brothers and a sister. The farm was sold outside the family
during the war.

On a chilly fall day, they take her parents and a sister,
and the kids, of course, to see the place. Her dad says
everything looks much the same. He means the same as
1943, the last time he saw it. He's hobbling toward the house,
stroke-frail, a daughter at each arm, and his gaze fixes on
the back porch. *I feel ghosts pulling at me,* he says.
For an hour or so, they imagine the long-ago: Clara
cleaning garden vegetables in the basement's big white sink;
Eric and Louie in the tool shed, its scalloped ridge cap
still there; her dad as young soldier walking unannounced
into the yard, home on leave to see his infant daughter.

As a girl, she used to stand at the edge of their farm and wonder about the Frost place just over the rise. Where had that storied road been? Her family's road. They make an offer on the original acres, not just on house and pasture, but Frosts turn them down. Only the ghosts can find their way from now to then.

Doorway

Summer daylight falls through the open door, and her father blinks. He's in his wheelchair. *Oh,* he says, *I thought we were at the farm.* He forgot he moved to town, a year ago now.

Moments before, the three of them sat together in the living room: she, mother, dad. During a pause in the conversation, her dad pushed up and out of his recliner. He wanted to go outside. She sprang up to help him. *No,* he said, *I want to walk on my own.*

He put out his arms, to keep her and her mother away. He seemed angry. They stood in the middle of the floor, the clock over the desk ticking in the silence. He took a step toward the wheelchair. They helped him into it. Once settled, he said to the floor, *If it was a switch, I'd turn it off.* No, you wouldn't, she thought, the anger jumping from him to her. That's when she opened the door.

Out on the front porch, they watch a gust of wind swirl a candy wrapper down the street. Two boys on bikes ride by. No one speaks.

That night she dreams of white birds in a dark sky, so high she can just see them, light-dazzled, as if a door somewhere stands open. A ringing telephone awakens her. It's her sister: their dad is in the hospital. As she dresses, she sees him in her mind, sitting at her mother's dinner table, here at the farmhouse, his face and arms brown with a farmer's tan. He leans back with a sigh, smiles, and with a touch of mischief says, *It's a sin to feel so good.* His ghosts have to drag him to the other side, just as she knew they would.

There Comes a Time

There comes a time
when night falls on us
and stars grow cold.

Thy Kingdom come
Thy will be done
on earth as it is in heaven

but stars don't sit in heaven
and their power and glory fade.

There comes a season
when stars are only stars.

Grief's Edge

Upon entering the empty house,
she sheds her jacket, lets her eyes
settle on her father's chair, soiled where
his head once rested. She sits
on the couch to wait. Soon

her mother opens the kitchen door.
Because the house is small,
the mother can see her daughter
but says nothing, sets down
a bag, her purse, keeps her coat on,
drifts into the dining room, grasps
the back of a chair, gazes down
as if she stands at the edge of
a great hole, a dark well.

Into the well she says,
I drove home on back roads
and turned where I thought I should
but everything looked wrong—
fields, trees, even the sky. Words
choke her. *I felt so lost,* she whispers.

The landscape tricks them both,
shifts each turn toward winter.

Sunday Chores

High on a wooden ladder in December, he feels like the
roof gutters he cleans, jammed with whatever falls from
the sky. What with farm work and his new full-time job,
Sundays are the only days slated for house chores.
He scoops up debris, drops it to the ground.

His thoughts wander. He saw a fox over by the trailer-
house yesterday. It must live in the creek. He should warn
the renters. The fox may be what's killing the farm cats.

He climbs down, moves the heavy ladder, climbs
back up. His thoughts resume. Their renters are good
ones. The first renters weren't. He doesn't like being a
trailer landlord, doesn't like not owning the farmhouse,
either. His wife says she feels like a child again, living in
it, though he knows she loves it. The rooms are open and
sunny. They could afford to buy only forty acres of farm
ground to help his in-laws move into town.

A black cat sharpens its claws at the foot of the ladder.
He looks down and says, *You'd better be careful, Blackie,
or Stormy, whatever the kids call you. There's a fox close by.*

With his next handful of debris, he realizes he's
holding black soil. A miracle. Dead leaves come alive
again. Taking off his glove, he scoops some more,

cradles its moistness, smells its richness, his mind going still. Winter sun warms his hand as he trickles the soil onto buff-colored grass. When he returns to task, he sees the clean half of the gutter and the good he's been doing.

The Land

Mule or machine
helped us take from her
what we needed,
what we still need—

farmers,
children of farmers,
grandchildren of farmers.
Remember?

We kneel on her,
dance, lie prone.
She takes us in,
makes us one.

The A-C 190XT

Big and orange, it was a lemon
of a tractor, needed repair
after repair, and then
the rear end went out.

He still sees it along the drive,
waiting for the winch truck, dumb
in its oil-stained brokenness.
This, after his father-in-law
died and an elderly landlord
took away ground, gave it to
a nephew. His other landlords
haven't followed suit. Not yet.

His wife works part time, and
he works full time and farms
evenings, weekends, holidays,
even vacations. He needs
a better job, needs to quit
the farm. Maybe he's
dug his hole too deep.

It haunts him, that tractor,
sitting there, broken.

How It Is Right Now

The Salina Journal
Sunday, August 3, 1986
Farm foreclosure facts don't reveal human tragedy

The words line up across the newspaper
like cattle at the feed bunk, bawling.
The two large pictures just above the fold—
portraits of farm widows, celebrity-like—
pull us in, each story boxed in thin black lines:

> ***Romance with farmland ended***
> ***after husband committed suicide***
> (Wyoming)
>
> ***Husband's suicide leaves widow***
> ***to fight to stay on ranchland***
> (Nebraska)

The second story in particular stays with us.
We picture the widow, last January,
hanging her kitchen calendar, imagine her
trying not to think about anything,
certainly not about her husband
leaving the kids Christmas gifts
before he put the rifle to his head.

But there, in a calendar square,
her square, *her* agenda, sits an entry
written in his hand. She lifts the page—
February, then March—and sees
banknote deadlines, calving dates,
a reminder to call about a pasture.

His granddad once owned the land, and readers
can gather the rancher bound himself to it
like a preacher to his parish. Face to page,
we want to shout, *It's only soil and grass.*
What about your wife, your children?

It haunts us, that calendar.
We can see it there over the table,
smell the ink of calculation, the blood.

Apart from Everything Else: Migraine

Her children can't know what to expect. Will their mother be reasonable, or sick and aggrieved, her words sharp like claws? They seem surprised when she snarls from a shadowy corner. Mr. Hyde evidently doesn't dominate. This is small comfort.

It begins with twinges, an ache behind the eyes. At its hammering pitch, it brings her to her knees, to sickness, to tears. When she's released, she's nothing but blankness, like Dr. Jekyll must have felt when he awoke in his lab, himself again but diminished.

Somehow she poisons herself. Do hormones cause this? Why would Mother Nature torment this way? Like hail smashing ripened seed, like the blister of lightning strikes.

She can't know this yet, but the headaches will eventually ease altogether. A bitter taste will linger, however. She'll never be able to fill that blankness, erase those Xs on the calendar. Her grown children will many times ask: Where were you?

Her husband asks

how she feels. He means,
does she have a headache?
Today she's fine and for

a sweet time that night,
they exist without question,
without thinking. There's only

touch   a yielding
a drop of gold into liquid glass.

Amid Blessings

> *...in Wildness is the preservation of the World.* - Thoreau

Wildness is precious measure
to hidden trials. It abides,
caring only to drink and devour,
sire and conceive, sprout and root.

It scurries, drones, lopes,
among rows of planted crops,
in tree lines, creeks, ditches.
In the soil seeds wait: stickers
and morning glories, thistle
and cedar trees, and grass—
blue stem, buffalo, switch.

We, who plant the crops
and dig the ditches, shape
the valley's legends, flaunting
our skills and whimsy. River
and hills fasten its treasure.

Who Will Listen?

The speaker, a weathered man, lectures before a scattering of townspeople. With practiced ease, he describes wastelands in Egypt and China that once fed empires. From there he touches upon Descartes, his error in breaking down truth, formulating certainty, no matter the place, the person. He then evokes the plains of Kansas and guides his listeners to the root of his talk: perennial crops. Words drop like seeds. *Prairie,* he says, *must be prairie. Crops must grow like the grasses.*

The man looks at her husband, the only farmer in the room, and nods at the cap on his head. *Logos,* he says, *for engineered products the farmer is told he can't do without are always placed strategically over the frontal lobe.* Everyone chuckles. The man grins. *The farmer isn't the problem, though*, he continues, *the paradigm is: agriculture-as-we-know-it doomed us centuries ago. Our salvation lies in place and people. Let the place teach the people.*

Her husband speaks up: *Give me the seed. I'll plant your crops.*

The man nods. He understands farmers are willing, but his mixed perennials—greenhouse designed, field-grown and monitored—aren't ready yet.

Nothing worth doing, he cautions, *can be done in a lifetime.*

That night, his words pester, coax her out under a vast sky. Brush rustles in the dark. A possum? Deer? *Let the place teach the people.* Her family has spent three lifetimes farming on the prairie. *What have we learned?* she wonders. *And if we know and say, who will listen?*

Prairie Eventide

Stars fling themselves
with such abandon we celebrate
the heavens, gaze into the deep,
cast our need like a net.

We listen for angels to rally
and long for goodwill to descend,
to shimmer like stardust and bind
sky to earth: hawk to vole,
rain to river, ash to the grass
from which it rises. We ask

salvation to rise with the moon,
unveil the night and this rolling land,
bend its light upon our heads
so we may see each other.

Weed Trouble

He couldn't keep up with the cultivating, not with his off-farm job. Over summer, pigweed grew along with the soybeans, so did elephant ear, while foxtail crowded the edges of the fields. A menagerie of weeds. All because he cut down on chemical herbicide in an attempt at something healthier than *agriculture-as-we-know it.* Daylight drained away in a run-off of hours, and now weed seed feeds into the combine reel along with the beans. He hasn't played it smart.

Bank examiners always play it smart, pluck weeds wherever they spot them. Just this fall, they yanked one of his scrawny bank notes. It's for the trailer-house, which isn't worth what's loaned against it. The banker knew this five years ago, but he'd been helping them put in the well and septic tank, thinking he'd get paid back when their house in town sold. That took over a year, and they didn't get as much as expected. Add the fact they lost their first wheat crop to hail, and he has to admit they left the banker vulnerable. The auditors have declared the note off the books: the bank takes a partial loss on the principal, and he can't list the interest as an expense, though the trailer is a rental. What the examiners can no longer see won't stick to their polyester pants. No cockleburs for them.

He sits in the creaking combine, feels a tug on his pride, just a little.

Balancing the Ledger

The combine rolls away, reel rumbling,
pheasants scattering. Her son grins from
the cab and waves. She waves back,
wondering why her husband is always
cutting soybeans on her birthday.

Her daughter skips ahead of her
and at the old corral dashes for home.
A gust of wind follows, stirs a patch
of yellow in the big elm by the house.
There's a sigh, almost as if something
speaks. *I'm here*, it says, *know me.*

She hadn't planned on marrying a farmer.
In truth, she didn't. Family turned him into one.
Her mother vowed, as a girl on the farm,
she would never marry a farmer, but
she did. Her aunts escaped, one as far as
California. She smiles to herself, hears
her dad's voice, an ease to it, riding
the chilly air: *Now is the time to balance
the ledger, and put the fields to sleep.*

The halting pulse of the back storm door
pulls her from her thoughts. It's as if
a spirit enters the house—a girl
wanting supper and a piece of cake.

Of an Autumn Afternoon

From an abandoned heap in the yard
children carve sand into a mountain—

They sculpt a shadowed cave
and a grand staircase, straight
and steep. They fashion sticks
into railings, plant root-torn grass
just so, on a ledge, in a hollow.
Cars and trucks appear (and roads),
a swimming pool (Barbie's),
and a lodge made from bricks.

Brother and sister barely speak.
They know what they want.

What sifts down inside them:
shared grit on fingers and knees,
scent of sand and leaves,
the cry of a circling hawk,
once and then it's gone.

Sometimes truth

clings like sand
and even when time

sweeps it away
and only a grain of it
lodges inside

we keep it close
because it's ours

The Supplanter

Was it an instance of intuitive foresight when her dad
chose her name, and her mom agreed? *Jacqueline,*
Old French, The Supplanter. She became the daughter
who married the man who would be farmer, and, in
so doing, supplanted her mother in her own house.

Her mother has lived in town for three years now, but
still misses the farmhouse, wind in the windbreak, the
quiet road. She knows this because a sister told her.
And being who she is, she can see only one answer:
to step out of the way.

Her husband, with help from family and friends, now
builds another house, in the backyard where her dad's
bachelor uncle once lived. The one-room shed is gone.
Should she say, supplanted? The new house is grander.
Drop-sided like a barn, stained red. The sale of cattle
(a gift from his parents) started them off, a charge
card keeps them going.

Mother is firm about not selling the place on contract.
Land keeps her settled. She will help with farmstead
expenses, they will contribute labor. She, the daughter,
shrugs off the fact—after all, it was her idea—this is
another temporary arrangement. She finds herself
listening to the cottonwoods, like her mother must
have. Their murmur grows into a rush of sound.
Thoughts flicker there, cooling themselves.

Where a Familiar Ache Rides

Wind sweeps across
silvery treetops, the quiver
like tumbling water.

It knocks at windows,
and at night wraps itself inside
our dreams. Tatters skitter

over the hills, and we savor
the ripple and pitch, the fury.

Half Bitter, Half Sweet

Two trucks move down the driveway, each pulling half
the trailer-house, opaque plastic masking its rooms.
He can't help but remember what Andy Rooney asked
a few years ago on the news show *60 Minutes: If mobile
homes are so mobile, why don't they get up and go?*
Well, Andy, theirs has gotten up, and is at least on its way.
Good riddance, he thinks. The couple who bought it can
have it.

He stands at one end of what is now empty space, near a
Russian olive tree, its scent half bitter, half sweet. The tree's
silvery leaves once shaded his baby girl's window in
summer, at bedtime. He can almost see her, grinning in her
crib. Her brother, cheeks flushed, waves from across the
years, from down the hall that's almost there again. Beyond
is the kitchen where he kissed his wife before he left for the
fields; and beyond that, the big living room where they all
gathered around the woodstove in winter.

Yes, he laughed when he heard Mr. Rooney say what he did
about mobile homes. But now it seems a little harsh. The
trucks pull onto the highway, head on down the road. He
watches until they're gone.

Taking Note

The summer before her mother came home they had
the disastrous wheat harvest. It was nineteen eighty-nine.
February weather swung from a seventy degree day to
subzero temperatures the next. In spring it hit a hundred,
and rain was scant. Dirt from miles away rode the wind.
Then the storms wouldn't stop, and weeds came on.
Old timers had never seen such dismal yields. It's true
most farmers had subsidized crop insurance, but that isn't
to say they didn't feel the seams of their pockets unraveling.

By coincidence, or maybe by a thread already stitched, her
husband got his old job back that year, the good one in
town. She became the farm accountant and co-business
manager and marveled over how little she knew as a child
about the business of farming, how little she knew when
she agreed to the takeover of the family farm.

Another note about that year: Her mother sold every
kernel of wheat that was hers and spent the entire sum on
a table-top Swedish Christmas tree. During the holidays,
she places it on the living room table, sets blue candles in
the pine sconces trimmed in red, steps back and says with
a glimmer, *My 1989 wheat harvest.* Behind this ritual,
buried deep, is a scythe-edged recognition: something
pretty makes a gift to the Fates.

Something More

Cottony tufts of seed
float by the window, distract her
from her work.
They rise
then fall
on air so gentle it's nothing

but sigh. Something
eludes her, something driven
not by calculation,
but by countless delicate seeds
drifting   drifting—
Hidden currents

merge
with the green
of low limbs, perfume
of dirt and grass, afternoon's
warm breath. Words
abandon
then catch her—
Here is the tease of poetry.

A Certain Solace

"So," Doris says, offering me another cookie, "your daughter's in college now." Cookies and coffee are farm-program-sign-up ritual. She continues, shaking her head as if what she's about to say is hard to believe, "And your son's getting married. I remember when they were little. They were so cute. You were a cute kid too."

We sit at her kitchen table. She picks up an ink pen and prepares to sign the papers, her arthritic hands resting over all the red Xs. She doesn't sign, she talks. "I remember Louie saying once how well you four girls got along. You were his favorite." Great Uncle Louie, gone now for so long. I may have been his favorite for only that day or month or year, but it pleases me to hear it.

When at last the papers are signed, coffee drunk, cookies eaten, we both walk to my car. Doris tells me she loves me, words she probably ends a phone call with, to one of her daughters: "Goodbye, I love you." But because she's never said them to me before, I have this impression she means Louie loves me, through her, because she thought to share his words. Driving home I picture him: a small man, bald, wearing wire-rim glasses, clad in denim overalls, smelling of tobacco and Luden's cough drops. He'd give us girls each a nickel or maybe a candy bar or, if nothing else, a cough drop, when we came to visit him in his little house across the yard.

She stops writing and glances at the clock. It's time to start supper, but she doesn't want to let go of her thoughts: if her husband hadn't chosen to farm family ground, she never would have known Doris the way she does now, or any of the elderly farm-landlord widows, including her mother. She returns to her notebook.

Today, Louie's words spring up like surprise lilies, like the ones from many years ago, sprouting and blooming in mid summer when I didn't even know they were there, only this time I don't feel them odd. I feel a certain solace.

To Have and to Hold

The farm couple thinks
their son too young to marry
or to farm for himself.
He should first learn
to pay the bills, study more
on how to hold onto dreams,
especially on the prairie.

After the honeymoon
but before days scatter
to the wind, his mother writes
the newlyweds a letter.
Give it thought, she says,
before you bind yourselves
to a farm. Those cords
can tangle and knot, or
come untied, especially
now, when costs are high.

Her words, more telling than
her own mother's had been,
are left to lie like grain
on new-broke ground. Rain
and sun will do the rest,
and wind. Always, the wind.

Deep in the Afternoon

(a note to the little ones)

Cedars hush the wind, here
in the cemetery. You want to run
among the stones. We won't let you.
Instead, you pick up sand,
sun-soaked, fold the pebbles
snug in the palm of your hand.

Great-grandmas and granddads
walk with us. They dwell within
chiselled names, old, familiar.

You crouch to study the ground
and they bend over you, hooked
like wings. Together you fingertip
pale grass feathered with seed.

Place and People

Autumn air drifting through open windows mingles with the smell of popcorn. Sisters, hair tinted, hands freckling, talk around their mother's table.
Their mother sits with them, a little hard of hearing, resigned to what's been agreed upon. She will sell the farm on contract to her third daughter and husband and become renter in her own home.

The talk turns to Bridgeport, the village where their childhood church once stood, before it burned down one December, embers flickering in the snow.

Remember Milo Gilberg? I thought she'd been named
  for the crop.
I did too. I liked her name.
We could call you Alfalfa.
Very funny.

Strangers live in most of the town, a mere cluster of homes in the middle of the Smoky Valley. Farm families have dwindled. Some old names live only in stone in cemeteries, and in the memories of those visiting around dining tables.

Sunrays slant through the windbreak, shadowing the wide front yard, lighting up prairie grass in the little pasture across the road. Something deeper drifts through the windows. The sisters look out, say how pretty it looks. Mother sets out supper.

December's End

Her mother stands over a box of stars and angels
in the west bedroom upstairs, the one
with the attic door. She's putting away
Christmas, face pale, mouth pulled down
like a bulldog, eyes troubled. She's missing
something, a wise man, maybe, or a shepherd.
That's the day everyone first sees it—
melancholia tinged with angst. She
thinks she's being cast off, left behind.

Next Christmas family carries on
as if nothing has changed. They gather
at the farm, bring crock pots of soup,
gifts for the tree, bottles of wine.
They never find what she lost—wise man
or shepherd. They still can't say what it was.

Ice Storm

A tree branch snaps in the gloom,
the sound like the crack of a rifle.
It clatters against the barn, glazed
power line caught in its tangle.
Nothing else stirs, including her.
Bundled in coat and scarf, she stands
in awe of this fantasy landscape—
Lewis' Narnia where it's always winter.

Her mother's house—the one here
on the farm, this dark icebox—
stings the back of her head.
It's empty. No, not empty.
She's moved her own things in—
they have, her husband and she.
Some boxes stand unopened.

I feel like I've died—Her mother
said this last spring, after family
moved her from farm to town.
She has her things, writing desk,
brass bed, red chair, but she
knows she's been left behind,
buried in white-walled silence

Snap—another branch.
Ice shatters in little pieces.

When Stars Are More than Stars

They pierce night with glimpses
of glorious dawn, explosions

out of darkness. We witness
icy void set afire forever
and ever. Without stars

earth would be nothing,
we would be nothing.

Here is love—
green sprout
heron skimming the water.

New Year's Day Hike at Kanopolis

A sharp wind slaps their faces, and one of them stops
along the rocky path to wipe a drippy nose. The entire
hiking group halts, gray sky muting colorful coats,
scarves, hats. The prairie opens before them; beyond
it, the frozen lake.

Moments before, he'd been remembering his Converse
tennis shoes from years ago, the ones he wore on his
honeymoon hike in the Guadalupe Mountains.
He's much better shod now, and in better shape too,
though he's almost sixty. He backpacks in the Colorado
Rockies every summer with kindred spirits. The Louise
Erdrich quote his wife likes to use pops into his head:
*What men call adventure usually consists of the stoical
endurance of appalling daily misery.*

Laughter begins to spread among the hikers, about the
insanity of tramping through this glacial afternoon.
Think hot shower and cold beer, he tells those closest to him.

Wind skips along tips of winter brush as they start again,
and his thoughts return to the mountains. It's true, he
suffers every summer: rain, wheezing lungs, aching joints.
But what's also true: a mix of camaraderie and solitude;
early morning fog giving way to sun-tipped peaks,

mountain upon mountain; night's stars, so many of them, an abundance of ice diamonds. Time banks itself and needs nothing from him. He can go home again to alarm clocks and all that sowing and reaping. Mountains, stars, kindred spirits. And the first day of another year. He can drink to that.

Homebound

The nursing home attendants settle the mother in her bed. She's old and frail, tiny, hair as white as the pillowcase. She beams at her daughter and says, *They told me I'm one of their favorites.* She seems childlike, like she did the day before at the hospital when she fussed at the nurse, as if she had no idea why she was being poked with a needle.

A week before, while in her wheelchair soaking up sunlight outside the rambling brick building, she talked of her childhood in the 1920s, of Saturday evenings when the family—parents, brothers, sisters— left the farm for the little prairie town of Roxbury. On those evenings, while her dad shopped at the general store, her mother visited Grandma Brown who ran the town's telephone switchboard from her tiny living room. Other women stopped by too, to hear the gossip. When it was time to go, the kids would pester their dad about ice cream. Did he have it? Maybe, he'd say, maybe not. If he had it, its paper carton would be tucked with frozen meat from the meat locker and hidden in the cab of the truck, at his feet, most likely. They'd ride home among the practical goods, eyeing each other, giggling, sun low in the sky, air and earth damping.

In her bed at the nursing home, she drifts to sleep. Morphine is started that evening. She dies four days later. After the Lord's Prayer at the cemetery, the daughter places a hand on the cool, burnished coffin. There's regret in the touch, for so many things, but most of all for death's loneliness. It isn't until later a final blessing springs to mind: May there be both farm and village in heaven, and long summer evenings with ice cream before bed, and, most of all, may there be family.

Precious with History

Sky like our mother's summer phlox,
our father's shirt one Easter,
arcs high over pastures and ponds,
ripened fields, peaks of barns—

tableau of a known world
brushed in tender strokes.

How small we are—
seeds packed with want,
fragile in our unfolding.

Rotating Fields

Willing to plant the next generation earlier in its season,
she's agreed to sell the farm to their son and his wife.
The son plans a bigger and better machine shop, the
daughter-in-law will make the red house into a studio, and
three granddaughters will settle into the farmhouse, the
two little ones scattering toys underfoot.

Today, sorting through things in her desk, reflecting on
the task of letting go, she comes upon a spiral-bound book
she must have thrown in the drawer years ago, a teacher-
assigned memoir written by their then junior-high-aged
daughter. She opens it at random and reads: *By age ten, I
kept a diary and wrote poems about things I couldn't tell
my friends. In a way, a pencil became my best friend.* Their
second child. She followed another family path, one that
led to the arts and education. Their daughter has tended
many a child, like she tends her summer garden, with the
faith of a farmer.

Setting the book aside, she pulls from the drawer the next
item, a collection of little maps drawn on a single piece of
paper: their landlords' fields, and their own. Her husband
made the original maps at her request long ago, making
it easier for her to pencil in acres, yields, rotations.
Alfalfa before milo then soybeans then wheat.
She may have kept track of fields better than she did
her children. Children are wildflowers, capricious,
tenacious, and sometimes a nuisance. She smiles.

A picture of the kids springs to mind, when they were little, with the grain elevator in the distance.
They stand on plowed ground and look as if they've sprung from the earth. She hopes they remember how they made the farm their own, how it fed their resilience.

Morning Coffee

The old fox understands the trap. – Unknown

They sit in the glider on the screened-in porch of their house in town, warm mugs in their hands. Birds sing. Trees bud.

Do you ever feel like the farm trapped you? she asks.
I wasn't able to farm the way I wanted to, he says, *but, no, I don't regret farming, if that's what you mean. If we had ended up somewhere else, something bad might have happened, like a car wreck as we were driving home for a visit.*
She's heard this argument before. *Yes, I know. Farming brought us here, to a charming little town in rural Kansas, which we like, a lot.*
I admit, he continues, *we didn't know what we were getting into, kind of like our honeymoon hike.*
Our honeymoon hike?
Did I ever tell you I was hoping you'd give up?
You were hoping I'd give up? Her voice rises a little, as if she can't believe her ears. *I was hoping you'd give up.*
But if we had, he says, *we wouldn't have stumbled upon that amazing forest.*

She steps again from the desolate side of a desert mountain into a cathedral of pines. Just as vivid in her mind: the slide back down the mountain, New Mexico sun beating on her, white dust in her nose, loose rocks threatening to fling her on her ass.

I had such a headache, she says.
I bought Absorbine Junior, he says.
This is our marriage, it seems: a contest of wills.
And look where it got us.
Yes, look where it got us.

They lift their mugs in salute. Hiking. Farming.
Marriage. It's the feat endured that matters.

Epilogue: Cottonwood 2018

The cottonwood towers above her where she sits at its thick base. Nearby, a clump of dead goldenrod, a beetle scurrying over littered ground. Warmed by afternoon sun filtering through bare branches, the creek smells of childhood.

She recalls a time when she, her younger sister, and two cousins, both boys, carried her dad's ladder down to the creek and propped it against the cottonwood's silvery trunk. The oldest cousin, around twelve years old, clambered up the ladder and into spreading branches. He couldn't get back down. His brother ran to the house to get her uncle, who then had to climb into the tree and help his son overcome his fear. *Just because these branches held you, doesn't mean they're going to hold me,* he said. He wasn't happy. They both made it back down with no mishap, but she remembers everyone's silence, each waiting for a branch to snap, bodies to fall.

A scurrying squirrel brings her back to the present. She looks up and into thick arms reaching into bright prairie sky. The cottonwood's size suggests an age of 150 years, maybe older. It's possible it was a sapling at the time of the Homestead Act of 1862. Native Americans still burned the prairies then, to keep them clear of trees so buffalo herds could graze. Her husband, a history buff, told her there probably were no trees along the creek bed in the early 1860s, except maybe this one, which could have taken hold at the same time a Swedish immigrant laid claim to this piece of ground.

Cottonwoods usually only live for seventy to eighty years. Why has this one survived for so long? Will it last much longer? Will the farm? She knows it's silly to tie the two together but she can't shake the thought that the death of the tree could also signal the final blow to the family agrarian era, just as its early survival signaled the end to the Native American way of life. Their son struggles even now to build the farm back into a viable business, but—to borrow from her uncle—the branches that held his ancestors may not hold him.

In the here and now, the big tree is alive, sap oozing. And the farm is alive, after more than a hundred years of family dwelling within its seasons. As if on cue, a child's voice weaves itself into the creek's invisible rustle. Her husband and granddaughters are crossing the bridge, coming to find her. She stands and waits, fingers slipping into the tree's rough, deep furrows.

Jackie Magnuson Ash grew up in Saline County, on a medium-sized farm, surrounded by a family of readers. After a college education, she expected to weave the written word into the fabric of marriage and children. The passing years gave her more than she could have imagined. She's been published in various journals and magazines, including *PlainSpoken: Chosen Lives, Chosen Words, Kansas Voices (2000-2004)* and Caryn Mirriam-Goldberg's *Begin Again*, an anthology of Kansas poets. She currently lives with her husband in Lindsborg.

This project was made possible, in part, by generous support from the Osage Arts Community.

Osage Arts Community provides temporary time, space and support for the creation of new artistic works in a retreat format, serving creative people of all kinds — visual artists, composers, poets, fiction and nonfiction writers. Located on a 152-acre farm in an isolated rural mountainside setting in Central Missouri and bordered by ¾ of a mile of the Gasconade River, OAC provides residencies to those working alone, as well as welcoming collaborative teams, offering living space and workspace in a country environment to emerging and mid-career artists. For more information, visit us at www.osageac.org

Osage Arts Community

www.ingramcontent.com/pod-product-compliance
Lightning Source LLC
Chambersburg PA
CBHW030131100526
44591CB00009B/600